While Walking in the Way of the Word

A book of big truths wrapped in a small package

Gretchen C. Nelson

Psalms 19:1-7

While Walking in the Way of the Word
© 2021 Gretchen C. Nelson

All rights reserved. Without limiting the rights under copyright reserved above, no part of this publication may be reproduced, stored, or introduced into a retrieval system or transmitted in any form, or by any means (electronic, mechanical, photocopying, recording, or otherwise) without the prior written permission of the copyright owner.

Acknowledgments

In remembrance of Carol Mitchell, a woman of the Word, my neighbor and best friend. She has now been given over to Eternity with Jesus. She is greatly missed.

With many thanks to Barb Schons and Colleen Wilts for their Tuesday visits; their prayers, suggestions, editorial and biblical knowledge.

Other titles by Gretchen Nelson include *The Camels are Coming* and *Mary: a Study in Luke 1 & 2*.

References to camels come from this writer's book: *The Camels are Coming* based on Genesis 24.

Printed in the United States of America

Introduction

Depending on the reason for taking a walk, much can be learned as we move ourselves forward one step at a time. Some of those walks take us into a forest of trees where we enjoy the scenery; some are an exercise for our health; some are just for the fresh air at a park. At some point these walks come to an end and we turn around, retracing our steps. But in the way of the Word, there remains another walk; one that is to be spiritual in nature. This is the walk of the Holy Spirit as He guides us in the way of the Word. No outdoors are needed; we might sit, walk, ride, or stand as He teaches and shelters us on the way. Neither is there a place for turning back. This walk is one of moving forward.

Occasionally, we read or hear of the term "walk of faith." While walking is a means of transportation, this walk doesn't require feet nor wheels to accomplish; it is rather a way of living in a believer's life. It is a time away from the noise of the world, a pause in the hustle of the world's doings, a time to think and pray with a Bible in hand.

It is also a time when the Holy Spirit offers something akin to physical walking and that is seeking the Word of God, its Truths and His will for our lives as we "take a walk" in that Word. It is having our spiritual feet guide us on a pathway expressly unique and designed for each believer with nary a map to guide our way. These "walks" are meant to teach and grow us in the Lord. It's a time of sanctification through testings, trials, disappointments, and hardships.

While walking this walk, another factor presents itself creating dangers in our spiritual growth and knowledge. These are the side pathways advertising another way, one with tantalizing fruit dangling from tree boughs. No matter the hunger-satisfying look, the enticing juice dripping from what could be lunch, we are to avoid that fruit. It's poisonous to our believer's walk. Perhaps wanting our familiar selves once again, we walk away from the Holy Spirit in order to take a short-cut to the goal, only to find our feet covered with mud. Even then, Jesus is with us as He washes the "sin" from self-propelling feet that had chartered their own course.

For a number of years, I fought and/or didn't know what was happening—usually looking at the disruption in my family and work life as an act of punishment. So I played the role of "I'm not going to go along with you, Lord" game. But I also wanted the milk and honey of the Word, so I chose Peter to read until it became startlingly clear in the passage of one verse. (1st Peter 2:1-3). I quit my "get me out of this" prayers and rested. Soon the Lord pointed me to another verse—this from Genesis 24:64-67. That was the shelf upon which I could hang my learning bonnet and invited the Lord to take me where He willed.

Up to that point in time, I had celebrated an on-going "birthday party" of sorts fashioned by the Lord. I was late in my understanding that these walks have purpose. And I was not a little disappointed that that phase of my new life was over. Those walks are works of trust as we face unwanted waves of hardships that seem to punish us rather than being a time of encouragement. However, the Holy Spirit has planned the perfect walk to unclutter the world from our beliefs. And it's usually a significant aspect of our being that He attends to first.

"To walk" (we do the walking in the Word), and "the way" (the plan of God for each who would receive it) (Jeremiah 29:11) work together leading to another factor the Lord desires in our lives and that is to rest in Him. The resting in Jesus is the giving up of our self-natures (which is difficult to do) allowing the Holy Spirit to guide us through the quiet of the Word so that no matter the negativity of life we are being led to rest our woes in Jesus.

First born into Adam's wilderness, these walks are meant for teaching, correcting, ridding the self of self, and a host of whatever the Holy Spirit sees as no longer needed nor wanted in the life of one living for the Lord. Though we walk alone, we've been entrusted with the task of shedding the sheaves of wrong that cling to our self-natures. It took a while to learn that these Word Walks are not just a few weeks' worth of learning, but something that is life-long.

One of the first lessons taught was that not only did the Bible contain Truth, but IS Truth. That which was Truth yesterday will be Truth today and Truth tomorrow. A second lesson was to learn the difference between Truth and something that looked like Truth, but wasn't and isn't Truth. It's receiving the gift and presence of discernment.

Reading the Bible, trusting its Truth, I began taking notes in its margins based on what was currently being experienced and learned, drawing lines connecting various biblical situations that I could employ for my betterment. Scattered and scribbled throughout my ancient Bible are learnings/Truths gathered while on walks in the Word. I found joy in making connections with passages that were thus applied to my life. I found that dozens of Old Testament accounts that matter in today's church are inside its covers. Warnings of listening to false teachers are sprinkled in the New Testament. There's even a passage concerning what a bad governmental leader will demand and ultimately do. (1st Samuel 8:4-22—giving them what they want; but not what's good for them.)

And we're never alone. By His Spirit, the Lord will bring alongside us as people of faith, sometimes from earlier biblical teachings that we remember and apply.

This is not a 1, 2, 3, "how to" type of book you've opened. These are truths/thoughts being shared from more than a half century's walk while "listening" to His Word. Though collected over a long period of time, they are still alive with meaning, needed and studied now in "such a time as this."

This book is intended to be of use for one individual or for small groups. Enjoy!

The Five Men of Faith

As we begin these spiritual walks, there often will be those who accompany us as we go. They don't actually walk with us, but by their teachings, they do. It's to these five long-ago men of God that I give a recognition of gratitude; men who gave their lives to the Truth of God's Word.

With the help from the teaching of these men, I started my walk. It's been (and will remain so) both coldly difficult, but also warm in its teaching of the Truth and bringing that Truth into my life. Under the umbrella of God's will and despite some "I can't continue on" situations, I've had a very rich life, one full of grace, God's love, surprises, healings, hills, valleys, adventures and a wonderful family.

PASTOR ED RICE: A former missionary, the shepherd of his flock, making certain no one was going to hell on his watch. He did that by teaching the Truth of the Word. We had to have our Bibles in our hands following along as the proof that he was preaching and teaching what the Word was saying. Every Sunday we were bathed in God's Word of Truth and its application in our lives. He was a man of prayer and his prayers had answers.

CHARLIE DOBSON: the Bible teacher, brought me face to face with 1st John 5:13, and let the Holy Spirit, through the Word, not by Charlie's explanation, do the work of implanting that Truth into my life. Nowhere but on the pages of Scripture do we find the face of God and I had been captured—wanting to know more than the Sunday School knowledge I possessed.

Pastor/Doctor Joe Knutson: His admonition when I started my journey down a wrong road: "Are you climbing up the rocky, cliff-hanging road to Mt. Sinai bursting with pride? Or are you walking up the pathway of God's Truth to Calvary's Hill where the Cross of Christ and death to self awaits?"

Pastor Maynard Force: A humble, uncomplicated man who spoon-fed the Word to the church with such ease and clarity, it was impossible not to listen to him. A small man, but mighty in the Word, he sat at my kitchen table between services, coaching me as a brand-new believer. He was one who knew the church of his time and saw where it was headed—to the church of today, these last days and the shaking it would sometime and positively endure. Fifty years ago, the church was already hinting at being divided between Truth and new truth, sorrowing this man of deep faith in the Word. Beside Pastor Force's antidote of "You must actually know the Word; you also must have discernment for the coming days. Not just skirting the edge of right, but Bible knowledge right." He also was a man who littered the heavens with prayer.

Pastor Richard Wurmbrandt: Speaking to a large crowd of people after the Holy Spirit had paid a visit to Southern California in the '50s and '60s, he asked the audience this question: "How many of you are filled with the Spirit?" Many hands went up and then he added "Which Spirit?"

That was a wake-up call that needed to be heeded. He also spoke of a coming purge of the church unless the Holy Spirit, not any old spirit, was allowed to be in attendance.

About four years later, we had moved from the area and membered in a relatively new mission congregation with two services. The visiting pastor (his first and only trip there) had a Word for the people (he not knowing that there was a current mini-battle concerning the Holy Spirit). The pastor's message summary? "Unless you allow the Holy Spirit to function in this church, the Lord will close the doors to this 'temple'." In a burgeoning community, and in less than three years, that church ceased to exist.

In the Beginning God Created
Genesis 1:1

The first biblical truth we learn concerning God is that there is no "was" to Him. He simply IS—always present—no matter what we consider to be time. He always has been and always will be "IS." Then we learn another truth: that He is powerful and beyond our comprehension to have created the heavens and the earth just by saying so with three words: "Let There Be." Furthermore, He "clothed" the earth with its miracles of beauty, provision, and a myriad of life support for those He made in His image and likeness.

In the beginning, in the nothingness of nothing, that which did not exist could not resist the power of God's Word.

_____

_____

_____

_____

_____

_____

_____

_____

Nowhere in Scripture do we read that God has forfeited the power He demonstrated in those first words. He still possesses that power and can and will use it at His discretion.

Not only do we find power in those verses, but Truth. No one can find another source for these beginnings.

Because He is still the creating God of creation, when a person agrees to walk in the Spirit, propelled by the Word of God, how many of those "let there be's" has one received as a gift and grace from God our Father? Seemingly coming out of nowhere.

In the beginning we also might see a "type," an example such as this: God created, Satan tried to disrupt, while the Spirit soothed the waters. (Genesis 1:1-3 and Colossians 1:13-17)

That same "type" is with us today. God's Word is taught; false teachers stir, mangle the Truth, and believing the false, people lose their relationship with the Lord. But in the end the Holy Spirit will bring a message of repentance which is to be accepted or rejected.

Satan, the Father of Lies, is a great imitator and uses positive words with a pinch of the false in his conversation, and quietly mixes at least one doubt in his words.

God is Truth; He cannot lie. Satan cannot speak Truth. His words are lies. But he does try to be sincere in his initial efforts.

We ALL have beginnings. No matter the country into which we were born; no matter the building of our arrival, no matter the arms that first hold us—we've begun. And we all have destiny—sometimes with the guidance of parent(s), sometimes by concerned pastors. Sometimes it's a birth into riches, sometimes into poverty, and sometimes, as we grow, we create our own destinies. However, for every one of those births there has been a plan developed by God the Father. (Jeremiah 9:11)

❧❦

It didn't take long to know what I wanted out of this life. However, and gradually, I became lost in Adam's wilderness of sin until the Holy Spirit shined the light of the Truth of God's Word into my mind. I have found His life in mine to be much better than the one I had made for myself.

Early on in our walks of faith, we learn that while God, Himself is infinite, so is His Word.

❧❦

God's question in Genesis 3:9, "Where are you?" was not geographical in nature, but spiritual. In so many words, and through the years, He's asked that question of many people—including me.

Why does He ask that question? He LOVES us and wants to make certain we're not putting on a few tiny fig leaves of our own instead of walking over to the Tree of Life (Jesus) to ask forgiveness.

However, it's human nature to blame human nature. (Genesis 3:12)

Aprons aren't powerful enough to cover the greasiness of our sin, whereas the Lamb of God's bloodied garment of righteousness does have that power. Our "self-works" are worthless, while the blood of the Lamb of God covers all sin. (Genesis 3:7, 21)

We want our sins forgiven, but don't necessarily want to give up sinning.

Knowing God and knowing about Him are two different practices.

It hurts the flesh nature to "know" Jesus. It can't survive the fire of His purity.

The journey from "I will be like God" to "I will be God" is a very slick and short one, lacking any rocks in the road in order to help people slide right to the gates of hell. But just to that gate, allowing time for repentance.

Whatever in our selves is not submitted to the Lordship of Christ is subject to the counterfeit.

Being made into the image of Jesus is a biblical teaching; it doesn't happen by trying. It's a dying to self that benefits that "make-over."

The activity of trying to earn one's salvation is not a biblical concept.

Worship is more than reading a script; it is praising the Lord with one's whole heart.

One cannot proclaim or teach Truth if it doesn't first reside in the teacher.

We are free in the Spirit; we just must be careful as to which Spirit we are bound.

The Holy Spirit desires to invade every secret place of our existence in order to cleanse first and secure for Jesus second.

Whatever "faith-driven" teaching that removes the necessity for Jesus is not of God the Father.

Just because a church is popular and growing is not a guarantee that their gates are preventing the entrance of the jackals of heresy that await on the other side of the fence. Although these animals enjoy a bit of nibbling on Truth found outside, they favor the tasty lies which they regurgitate inside the gates later on. (Taken from thoughts in the Book of Nehemiah)

Philippians 3:10a "That I may know Him" should be my daily prayer, but I don't much care for the last part of that verse.

Listen to the Lord and die to self, die to self and again listen to the Lord, this must be my walk.

The end of myself, the beginning of God . . . but, I keep climbing out of the grave of death to self in order to pander that self.

Lazarus' story is proof that even when Jesus is late, He's always right on time.

Whenever we build upon a man's word, we have a dying religion. When we build on God's Word, we have relationship with the life of the Lord.

Obedience to the Word keeps us in the light; the more the light the more we see Jesus.

It isn't what we know; it's Whom we know that matters.

Like Mary in John 2:5, the church needs to do whatever the Son, the Word made flesh, tells us to do.

Too often I cover my guilt with sticky fig leaves rather than His beautiful robe of righteousness.

We serve the God Who overlooks nothing but oversees everything.

My relationship with Jesus must turn from what He does for me to Who He is.

Sanctification is a time wherein the Holy Spirit fastens us in His grip from which there seems to be little or no escape.

Sanctification is also a time of testing which cleanses our spiritual pores and when the trial gently comes to an end, we know we are living differently and believing more deeply.

The spiritual rest of God is putting everything into His hands—our illnesses, our worries, our fears, our woes, our fright. As we basically have more trust in ourselves than in an unseeable God, that's not easy.

In order to walk biblically, not stumbling or falling, we first must be willing to open our eyes to Truth.

Life is a journey with two forks in the road: One is labeled "The Truth," the other "The Lie," and the lie is too often too fetching to lay aside.

The reason that so many churches are powerless is that they have refused to die to the Adamic nature instead of rising to a newness of life which is being infused by the Holy Spirit.

In life, we don't know what we don't know until we know we don't know it. It's the same with our views of the Bible.

A pastor or teacher can only take a congregation's spiritual growth as far as s/he knows Truth.

A sermon is the revealer of where the speaker is spiritually. Thus, the bulk of a congregation lies in the throes of spiritual death if the Jesus of the Word isn't preached.

My vision had lain dead for many years until my "Lazarus," my problem, came out of its tomb and had no stink to it. A new life had been born in me.

In a time of extreme crisis, my prayers of doubt flew overhead like buzzards waiting for death to occur. Forty years later, the bird is dead and I'm living with more trust in Jesus.

There are times when we think that God doesn't care about a little bite of sin; it's the big sin that He won't tolerate. That thinking won't survive the Court of Christ.

Two differing prepositions determine an outcome: working FOR God or working WITH God. The former is legalistically driven to failure; the latter is "alongside of" wherein we enjoy His rest as He guides it all.

֎

The tenant of Christianity that we must hold tight, is the dual truth that Jesus lives in the believer and we died with Him on the Cross.

֎

※

Alas, as the bride of Christ we have the capacity to commit spiritual adultery.

Only an addiction to self impedes Holy Spirit activity in our lives.

※

In order to bring about His glory and a further revelation of Who He is, the Spirit can and will create a faith in us equal to the test of suffering we must occasionally endure.

If the Word of God is the only source of "seeing" God, then why do we leave it on the bookshelf?

≈≫

If we believe that we cannot be deceived, we already are.

≈≫

It is while in the hot desert pit like Joseph (Genesis 37:17-24), or hiding in the dark Engedi cave like David (1st Samuel 24:1-22), or sitting in the lion's den like Daniel (Daniel 6:16) that we are forged and shaped into the character of Jesus.

ରେଓ

One who declares being Christlike in life is demonstrating pride and a lack of Christlikeness.

Too often, it seems that I'm stuck between self-piety and Holy Spirit holiness.

ରେଓ

༄༅

We can tell what spirit resides in us by what we "feed" ourselves.

༄༅

Troubles in most forms are only vehicles giving us the opportunity to see the revelation of Jesus at its end. (Genesis 24)

Look up, not down during times of trouble.

Prayer is the vehicle we use to bring about God's will into our lives.

❧ ❧

When Jesus entered the darkened womb of Mary, He left no part of Himself in heaven. Who can fathom this truth? That's a work of faith. (Philippians 2:5-11)

❧ ❧

_____
_____
_____
_____
_____
_____
_____
_____
_____
_____
_____
_____

Jesus did not come to cure societal ills. He came to change the human heart which will then cure the ills.

The following was written in my Bible in 1983. "The Bible speaks of lost sheep; today we need to speak of lost shepherds."

Long ago the church became apostasy-ed; instead, it should be apostle-ized. Or is it too late?

Many come under the letter of the Word but remain outside the Spirit of it.

❧❧

When the Holy Spirit leads us into "rocky," difficult places, He has already "planted" the necessities for our survival. (1st Corinthians 10:1-4)

❧❧

I must never traffic in unfelt, unknown truth nor anything that is foreign to the Word.

Looking back at our miss-steps, decisions made, or lack of faith, how many of us wish we could start our lives over again?

We don't have to go through hell before arriving in heaven—neither figuratively nor in reality.

Because we are to be dead in Christ, the plea of "use me, Lord" is not a biblical teaching. It's soulishness.

Like the Jews of old who were taken to Babylon as punishment for not obeying God's Word, the church needs to know that having a strong historical past in the Word is no safeguard for remaining so in the currency of today.

It's very simple. Through belief in the finished work of the Cross of Christ, we are unleashed from Adam's sinful nature to be transformed into the image of Jesus.

A danger for any church body is when it seeks to grow wider in attendance numbers, but not deeper in the faith and knowledge of the Word of Truth.

The church and Jesus are not the same thing.

Bringing people to church is not necessarily bringing them to Jesus.

If a church body isn't being persecuted, dare it be called a church?

It is popular today to state that "Black Lives Matter." So be it; however, God's Word Matters more.

If we know and understand that Jesus is the Head of the church and we the body, wouldn't we be clinging to Him more earnestly and make certain we "do the work" of a body?

It is impossible to "cast out" the flesh nature. We must die to it: take its breath away.

God's call or a task to a believer is always intensely personal and backed by Scripture. It's best not to move forward without those verses of Scripture. It's spiritual failure and suicide.

When facing dark situations, it is best to wait for God to roll the stone away than to exhaust ourselves trying to chisel our way out of the problem. He sees from every angle and His timing is perfect.

God never asks for our opinion concerning His Word.

⋧⋦

"Sir, we would see Jesus" should be the cry heard in every church. (John 12:21)

⋧⋦

Our temptations often come alongside our abilities.

Lord, stretch my gaze to behold Your glory.

Our Lord is the God of the "more than enoughs." If I know that, why is provision the strange god to which I often bend my neck? Instead, I must bow to the Lord of the sparrow.

Only an addiction to self impedes Holy Spirit activity in our lives.

We like our Bethlehems where something new is birthed into us. However, we don't much care for Jerusalem where something in us must die. Both offer considerable pain.

※

Which holds the larger influence in my life: the I AM of God or the I am of self? I don't like my answer.

Brought by lie filled, snake covered visitor, Eve's bad choice had ramifications for all eternity; so did Mary's angel, speaking a Truth brought Word.

※

If the Lord put together the human body, why will He not automatically repair it? That's a puzzlement.

Lord, why did you create us with an inner vacancy, giving us the choice of filling it with the putrid emptiness of the world's garbage or the refreshment of Your Word?

It is amazing that while reckoning myself as dead how alive to the self I stay.

A difference exists between knowing one's self and dying to self. The former is ego building; the other is Spirit filling.

During times of trouble, I've often heard the cawing of the crow more loudly than the chirping of the sparrow.

‌ ‌ ‌ ‌ ‌ ‌ ‌ ‌ ‌ ‌ ‌ ‌ ‌ ‌ ‌ ‌ ※

If we want to be like Jesus, we must also bear His wounds.

‌ ‌ ‌ ‌ ‌ ‌ ‌ ‌ ‌ ‌ ‌ ‌ ‌ ‌ ‌ ‌ ※

We're all born of the flesh nature. At some point in time that nature will control us as the devil creates walls of futility. Futility is one of Satan's favorite party favors.

To state that a congregation is Christlike is like digging a hole from the bottom. Christlikeness is a work of the Holy Spirit and can't be purchased by good behavior.

⁂

We could pay some attention to the two water crossings seen in the Old Testament. If we turn those waterways into problems, most of us would take our flippers and run back to Pharaoh's sandwiches. We know what to expect in the way it's always been. It takes faith and courage to plant our feet and wait for God to part those waters for newness in life.

⁂

_____

_____

_____

_____

_____

_____

_____

_____

_____

_____

_____

Today, we're more interested in the fruit of life than the root of it. If the root is rotted, there will be no fruit.

If the basis of our beliefs is in error with the Word, we'll not blossom with the fruit of Jesus.

One who is mixed in Spirit, is also mixed in message.

Satan is no longer fighting the church; he's joined it, making friends with the vulnerable.

Many live in a Christian society in which it's enough to know one is saved, or hope to be saved.

It wasn't my decision to "rebirth" me. It was the work of the Holy Spirit—sort of like Mary—it just happened—as I read 1st John 5:13. I walked away—different.

❧❦

During times of spiritual famine, God examines our hearts. What or whom do we seek to fill our hungry souls? Upon whom or what do we rely? What satisfies us?

❧❦

Two thousand years ago, the church died to the right to herself. But too many of us have forgotten that fact.

Satan knows the Word better than the "average" Christian, and he often uses his interpretation to steer people in the wrong direction. It happened to the first woman. With so many temptations, it can currently happen to any woman (or man).

And who wants to be an "average" Christian?

There exists no works big enough, important enough, long enough, wide enough to use as a "ticket" into heaven. Only the blood of Jesus will suffice. And while on the cross, He already shed that.

What do we know of all that transpired on the Cross of Christ that day?

(Luke 2) The angel told Mary that ". . . nothing will be impossible with God." As we trod our walks in faith, we find that verse to be truth in our own lives—no matter the difficulty of putting one foot in front of the other, His promises will be fulfilled in their own time.

It's the ". . . will be . . .," the tomorrow of God's Word that Satan sometimes uses as a snare to focus our attention on the "not yet" and "won't happen."

In the '60s, I knew a few pastors whose lives had been impaled on the Cross of Christ. Their sermons were simple, full of the Word, and prophetic in nature. They also saw the bold beginnings of leakage away from God's Truth.

It was difficult to learn to trust faith in Jesus and not the coins in my purse.

The belief in "once saved always saved" brings a careless, unfruitful and self-reliant religion with it. (Colossians 1:21-23)

The seed of a parent gives us a first birth; while the Seed of the Word gives us our second birth. 1st Peter 1:23

In a liturgical service, stating that we are in bondage to sin is to confess that the cross didn't do its work.

Like the ancient tower of Babel, we also want to build big houses of worship using a vote of "Let us" as the assurance that God is with the project.

However, like Babel, whatever godless, self-sufficient, high thing we "let us" build today could find itself in a heap of rubble tomorrow.

※

Why is it that people seek the relics from the time of Jesus rather than the current offering of His righteousness?

※

I never like the vehicles the Lord uses to answer my prayers for being made in His image.

Faith is as strong as the test it survives.

A chasm exists between the preaching/teaching of information versus revelation. The first will get us across the street; the other has the Holy Spirit as the driver.

The Son of God became the Son of Man in order that the sons of man might become the sons of God.

When we nourish others with the Word, we are emptying ourselves of ourselves.

Two factors exist in Mary's statement of acceptance: "... let it be to me..." and "... according to Your Word." We like and desire the me part of her confession, but don't want to spend too much time with the "Your" factor. (Luke 1:1-38)

~~~

Believing God's Word today will bring blessings that stretch far into the future. (I've experienced that factor, more than once.)

~~~

_____

_____

_____

_____

_____

_____

_____

_____

_____

_____

_____

_____

The Holy Spirit's "job" is not necessarily to make bad people good, but to make the living dead come alive in Jesus.

What in my life needs raising from the dead? What point of darkness needs the resurrection power of the Lord? What impossibility needs His uplifting hand? (1st Peter 1:21)

"Abraham believed God and God counted it unto him as righteousness"—mentioned four times in Scripture. Believing God must be the umbrella under which we hold our faith.

Abraham went from listening to God to listening to his wife. (Genesis 16:1-6) For a moment in time he failed to trust his Lord. That's a common thread throughout people of faith. A problem hanging over one's head.

Ishmael: a portrait of what happens when the waiting for God to act becomes too anxiety driven on our part; so we find a way to bring that promise into reality, not caring what could be a negative outcome.

I've had a number of Ishmaels knock on my door and some I invited in. I wonder how many hands I'd need in order to count all my Ishmaels, planning my own way out of a problem or fulfilling a need, or not quite believing that God is a God of solutions and right timing. My latest Ishmael had a lot of fun riding the "camels" he found in our living room.

A true occurrence: It wasn't until I rid myself of "my own Ishmaels" that God fulfilled His Word's promise for my life. In less than 24 hours.

Righteousness is not a list of attainments. It is the blood-soaked blanket of the Lamb of Christ that God puts over the believer as a cover.

❧ ❧

Who among the church would dare to say to the Lord, "Do with me as you wish"?

❧ ❧

_____

_____

_____

_____

_____

_____

_____

_____

_____

_____

_____

Holiness does not require works of the flesh; instead it is God's gift through faith.

Obedience Obliterates Obstacles (Joshua 3:14-17) This life saving Truth was practiced and granted.

No longer do we live in a church setting wherein hearts on the outside of it melt and courage escaped by those who could actually destroy us just by their presence. (Joshua 2:11)

A "mature" Christian is one who is at rest in all things Biblical, knowing and trusting that the Lord has that person in His care.

Sometimes a fresh revival is nothing more than a flesh revival.

If the wreckage of Sodom and Gomorrah was an early picture of today's world, what character in that city would each of us be? I'm nosy and fear that I'd sneak a look back as did Lot's wife. However, I'd rather have sugar than salt.

And about other ancient communities: Noah built an ark with only one door through which to enter. Many teachings can be learned through that ark, but the major message given is that, like the ark, there is only one gate into heaven.

We can cast out Satan, but we can't cast out our flesh nature. It must die and it's difficult to rid the self of self.

Satan can't violate man's will, and God won't. Our wills are free.

I must put myself in a place where nothing else matters but Jesus' life in mine.

The flesh nature is a way of being with which we were born—a gift from Adam and Eve. Believers are given the opportunity to die to that nature, but there's always a bit of it left. Then that bit becomes the handle Satan uses to pull us away from Jesus.

Like the cover on an orange, our flesh nature must be "peeled" before the "fruit" of the Lord's character may be "tasted" by others. And some oranges are easy to peel, while others hang on to their fleshy covering.

A difference exists between Satan's accusations and the Holy Spirit's convictions. We need to learn the difference.

In the view of Jesus, there are only two races of people: saved into His kingdom by believing the "work" of Jesus on the Cross, and those who do not believe—yet.

We reflect that which we spend time looking at.

Even confessed sin haunts us. That's Satan's work. He enjoys stirring up what we had buried at the foot of the Cross. However, don't dwell in the event, take it to the Lord, and "hear" Him say, "What sin?"

Whatever happened to the word "carnal" coming from pulpits.

God doesn't "send" people to Hell; people go there because they refused the Alternative.

"What will be, will be" is a worldly cliché, not a spiritual principle.

In today's world, there seems to be a big difference between the heartbeat of God and the pulse of the church.

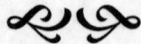

Pridefully telling God that he wanted to be God—like it was his turn—sent the beautiful being called Lucifer spinning out the gates of heaven, never to enter again.

Since his arrival on this planet, Lucifer/the devil has been busy fulfilling his number one desire, being "god" in a kingdom of his own making. That "kingdom" is one that teaches that "We're all gods."

The founding principle behind the teaching stating that we are all gods, had its beginnings thousands of years ago in the Garden of Eden and is now experiencing a return with the teaching of our "godhood" being taught even in some churches.

Remember, Lucifer is fairly dumb; so his favorite way to successfully exert himself is by going backward in time and copying it. (Genesis 3:1-6) Satan doesn't possess a deep, thinking mind; he's a copy-cat angel of deception. However, he needs watching, just in case.

※

As with Adam and Eve, the trouble with sin is that it very often has an impact on others. Sometimes for a very, long, eternally long time.

※

_____
_____
_____
_____
_____
_____
_____
_____
_____
_____
_____
_____

When I feel "unhinged" from the Lord with life just too difficult, I pray: "Lord, tighten Your grip on me, hang on to me, don't let go." I pray that even when I'm mad at Him.

Sometimes, we pay more attention to the powers that be than the POWER that is.

"But God" is one of the most powerful statements in the Bible. It confesses His sovereignty and often suggests change for the better.

❧❧

Our past doesn't need to determine our futures either in the secular or the spiritual world.

When the heart is given over to the will of God, it's a certainty that He will get the feet there also.

❧❧

Any "biblical" teaching that doesn't have Jesus at its core is false teaching.

Many years ago, after "reading" the signs of the times, we were warned by various Bible teachers that in the near future there would be a flood of false teachers. They were wrong; it's a tsunami of them.

In these last days, it is important for Satan to rid people of truth, filling them instead with the latest "new thing." That "new thing" is as old as sin itself. It's just wearing different "clothing" today.

Spiritually speaking, not all growth is good growth. Some of it is "cancerous" in nature.

A believer's life must be clean of clotted sin. Those clots build up in our spiritual veins, taking up space that the Lord wants to use for a clear flow of biblical revelation.

Being born again is not so much by making a decision of the flesh, but by the sacred activity of the Holy Spirit.

Eve and Mary. They each made a choice. Eve birthed sin into everyone ever born; while Mary birthed the cleansing Power of that sin into all who would receive it in that same world. Just two women; sort of odd to think about.

This worldwide pandemic is one of Satan's finishing touches before Jesus returns. He sees the writing on the wall and without the ability to read it, is digging deeper and wider into the church. Just in case . . . (Daniel 5:5-8)

Simply put, we have to die to the self-nature in order to live in the Jesus nature.

❧❧

Today's marketplace is full of "How to" books, usually based on how to make oneself a better self or how to discover our individual gifts. Makes one wonder what people read in 1179 to build up the self.

❧❧

⊱⊰

As I get older, I'm saddened to have wasted so much of it "scrubbing floors" while the Word awaited, ready to reveal its Truths.

⊱⊰

_____
_____
_____
_____
_____
_____
_____
_____
_____
_____
_____
_____

Being refreshed by God's Word in the early morning can be more refreshing than that first cup of coffee.

Reading the biblical letter to the Ephesians is more calming than soaking in a warm, sudsy tub of water.

~~~

If we are the body of Christ, shouldn't we be going wherever the Head goes? And believing what the Head believes?

~~~

❧❧

"Hail, oh favored one, the Lord is with you," greeted Mary one day. Wouldn't it be refreshing to hear that same welcome in church prior to the service?

❧❧

_____
_____
_____
_____
_____
_____
_____
_____
_____
_____
_____

꽃꽃

Any congregation with the acknowledgment that Jesus is God and the forgiver of our sin should consider ourselves as a one in faith. However, we like our independence, our pride filled sins and doing it our way. When He comes to get us, how is that going to look? "Take us first!" "Take us first"!

꽃꽃

Do we ever think of ourselves as having the favor of God? It isn't a feeling, but an acknowledgment of a fact. Maybe if we practice that Truth, we'll have a closer walk with the Lord.

❧❧

The only thing we know of Mary prior to that declaration was her impending marriage. What in her past made her a woman of favor? If we were to know, the Bible would have told us. We don't know because otherwise it would become a circus of "Who is Most Like Mary?" rather than growing in the image and likeness of Jesus.

❧❧

_____
_____
_____
_____
_____
_____
_____
_____
_____
_____
_____
_____

Whatever we seek in the flesh as a "help" for Jesus is doomed to failure.

It is sad that we are living in an era during which the tares are more popular and seemingly more refreshing than the sweet grain growing among them.

If, biblically speaking, we are the of bride Christ, why do we shun spiritual intimacy with Him?

In Genesis 1:26-27, we see that Adam was created in the "image and likeness" of God. Sin entered the couple and God, who loved His creation, needed a recompense which was His Son, Jesus. In Luke 1:33-35 we read of this event. Philippians 2:5-10, tells us the Truth of that occurrence. Jesus, forever in the body of a human, walked among the people. That is Love Incarnate. How can we refuse such love?

I'm but a vessel of the Lord; one with a number of leaky holes chiseled into it from the worries of life's woes. It could be said that I'm "built" with too many bricks and God chisels at bricks, but not at stones. I must allow more stones in my life.

The pandemic dictum of "no church" is a mandate fresh off the antichrist's computer.

Human sweat adds nothing to the work of Christ on the Cross.

A "church" that doesn't teach the biblical Jesus should call itself something else.

Whatever happened to anointed teaching?

Tolerance is an indifference to the Truth.

☙❧

If I cast all my anxieties on the Lord, all I have left is peace and rest.

☙❧

_____
_____
_____
_____
_____
_____
_____
_____
_____
_____
_____
_____

∽⚬∾

The saying that "God's in charge" is like stating that He is a puppeteer managing our strings. In reality, if any wrong occurs we then have Him to blame.

∽⚬∾

For good or not, our wills are our own.

What God promises in His Word He "delivers," just not necessarily on our time-table.

What do we do that gives the Lord pleasure?

When we behold Him, we become like Him. The beholding takes place in the Word.

I never want to erase the memory of a person who has left the imprint of Jesus in my life.

Praise is a tool for overcoming what assails us. It is the aligning of ourselves with the Host of Heaven.

When feeling lost and/or alone, turn to Jeremiah 29:11. No name is attached to that verse. Because He loves you, (and all the other you's on this planet), He's drawn plans to help along the way. A simple prayer asking the Lord to guide a person to a page in the Bible, would help in finding what that plan is.

Hell is the place of confinement, perpetual darkness, suffering, anger, fire, gritting what teeth are left, fighting, rotted food, and not one second of hope of ever getting out. It's eternal: never ending.

Heaven is a place of uninterrupted fellowship with the Lord, continuous glory, rest, disease free, perfect weather (if there is weather), worship, full of knowledge, with no competitions. But most of these are earthly situations. Heaven will be perfect for all residents. While on this earth, we're incapable of knowing the décor of heaven until we get there.

Trusting the Lord for eternal life is relatively easy. Trusting Him for life on this planet is something else.

Decisions determine destiny.

The Lord is slow to anger and abounding in steadfast love. (But don't push it.)

Strong winds of difficulties often come after an unexpected blessing. A vice versa is also true.

One who is mixed in Spirit is thus mixed in message.

"Going, they were healed." "On their way rejoicing." ". . . arose and went." How does the church of today apply these verses of Truth to the body?

It is difficult to teach Truth to one who is filled with the self.

Hundreds of years ago, Jesus was hidden away in Mary's body through the Holy Spirit's overshadowing power. Today, Jesus is hidden away by some pastors who don't quite know what to do with Him.

༺ ༻

Today, it's very popular to seek unity amongst religions. Ultimately, around what campfire will the finished product gather? Certainly not the Lord's. He's not fond of mixtures.

༺ ༻

༄༅

There never was a time when the Creator didn't exist. He never was not God.

༄༅

The 1st Adam died carrying sin in his back "pocket." The Last Adam also died, carrying our sin in His "spiritual pocket."

Forgiveness is not so much a remission of penalty as it is a restoration of relationship.

_____
_____
_____
_____
_____
_____
_____
_____
_____
_____
_____
_____
_____

The Christ of God is the Head. The Church is to be the body of Christ. Sadly, in many cases they've become disjointed.

❧❦

Doctrine and truth are not the same thing: doctrines vary; but Truth is Truth and cannot be varied.

If baptism with water saves, there's no reason for Jesus allowing Himself to be nailed to that Cross.

Another factor; if baptism is the means of salvation, why aren't pastors walking the streets with a hose?

❧❦

✦

When was the last time the people of God rejoiced with real, unutterable and exalted joy?

✦

Satan knows well how to use the text of Truth, twisting it ever so slightly, thus catching us in his net.

Faith is as strong as the test it survives.

Trying to be like Jesus is not a biblical concept. We are not meant to TRY, but to BE.

In regards to Satan, nothing is new under the sun.

In the 1980s spiritual growth was a big "churchy" topic. However, measuring growth has always been a grandma's purview. God hasn't given us a primer for spiritual growth. We'd make it another contest.

Currently, some are back at determining one's spiritual growth and abilities, this time with upscale tables of measurement. It's taken Satan a little over 40 years to come up with nothing new, just with other authors.

To know our spiritual growth only proves how much time we spend looking in a mirror.

We are all born in a wilderness of Adam's sin. The only way out is to ask Jesus the way to be "born again" as seen in the Word.

❧❧

Satan's methods are very shallow. He's not too smart, but he is sneaky, so he goes around in circles like the Israelites in the desert looking for someone to entrap. And he's also into keeping his style.

Satan is well aware of the value of Truth in the lives of people; but if he told Truth, he'd just be a nobody in their midst when he wants to be the "Big Guy," the leader, the know it all. (This is conjecture.)

❧❧

If I "swallow" the venom of the garden's snake in the morning, I can be assured that I'll be belching up the dragon's vomit that night.

Jesus, the Shepherd came to find lost sheep; some of today's shepherds need to find Jesus.

Many years ago, and in my lifetime, we were warned that the church would soon become apostacy-ed. In too many cases that happened. These churches need to be apostle-ized—back to biblical basics.

Trying to do something "for" Jesus is an example of the flesh wanting to be noticed.

The Spirit can and will create a faith in us equal to the test of suffering we occasionally must endure.

It hurts the flesh nature to "know" Jesus. It can't survive the fire of His purity.

If we seek being recreated in the image and likeness of God, we shouldn't be angry with God's means of getting us there.

When planting a garden, we put a seed into the dirt from which will grow a root and then the stems of fruit. That's a picture of the believer. The Seed of Truth is planted, a root of faith sprouted from Truth that will grow into food of the Word that can be shared with others. But people don't garden very much anymore.

❧❧

The Bible begins and ends with a reptile. (Genesis 3 and Revelation 20) They can be, will be, deadly.

What was no more than a beautiful snake in the beginning of the Word, morphed itself into a giant killer dragon at its end.

❧❧

The Lord hasn't asked us to cope but to overcome.

One old problem in Christianity is that we are bent on completing "work" that Jesus finished on the Cross.

※

In Exodus 17, we find that the Israelites had been circling the desert floor with this question in mind: "Is the Lord among us or not?" When the "going" seems unending and tiring, I've also asked that question more than once.

※

܀

I wonder how often I've not stepped aside in order to see and listen to a "burning bush" waiting to teach me more of Himself and His ways. (Exodus 3)

܀

Prayer is not so much a habit as it is a necessity.

If Jesus is the Bread of Life, why do I eat my breakfast toast before I read the Bread of my Salvation?

I never want to hear the words from Matthew 7: "I never knew you."

൞൞

I'm determined to live in the arms of faith not yoked to the stiffness of fear. It's easier said than done.

൞൞

The few days, months, years I have left, must be spent digging wells of truth from the Word in order to sate one who is thirsty. (Including myself) (John 4) I already have a shovel.

The Israelites did, I suspect we do also: When the Lord appears to be slow in responding to our prayers, we have a tendency to seek something to fill that void—something like building a golden calf.

Our spiritual DNA carries the stain of Adams's sin until or unless the blood of Jesus gives it a cleansing.

Mary is one to be studied, not worshiped.

I'm quite certain that Mary knew and felt His Presence. If Jesus lives in us, in me, why am I not conscious of that "Christ in me, the hope of glory"? How would I live differently? Talk differently? Witness more? (Colossians 1:27)

⁂

Will the church hide itself in the coming days? Or stand firm at the front door?

⁂

_____
_____
_____
_____
_____
_____
_____
_____
_____
_____
_____
_____
_____

Three practices come into view as words to live by: 1) Know the Father's will; 2) Submit to Father's will; and 3) Walk in Father's will.

How many in Christianity know how to tear down a stronghold occupied by Satan?

Truth in, truth from, and truth revealed in God's Word, not someone else's word, (including mine) is the saving factor for all people, all the time.

When life becomes impossible, the Holy Spirit will always point us to the Bible to help us through those times. Read it until something strikes home, fitting the difficulties we currently experience. The Holy Spirit will then give the courage to trust that at some point in time, the trial will be over.

Righteousness is not on a list of one's attainments.

The "deadly D's" in order of occurrence: Disappointment, Discouragement, Depression, Despair, Defeat. Before we get too far down that line consider Jesus and His love and care for us. And Christians, believers are not immune from these times.

If the fruit of righteousness isn't hanging from our branches, we're in spiritual trouble.

God's love is not measured by our response, but His life flow through us.

Touch and taste. (Mark 5:25-34) (John 4) Two women, one touched the hem of Jesus' cloak, the other argued a bit before "tasting" the "waters" of salvation He offered. Sometimes we touch the Lord through His word and sometimes we're wanting proof by His actions.

It's favorable to trade Facebook time for Jesus book time.

Once we've received Jesus into our lives, we have no right to ourselves. We belong to Him. And oh, the difference.

❧❦

The Trinity of God had never experienced death until the Man Jesus obediently went to the cross and willingly submitted to the power of death. Just for you and just for me.

❧❦

_____
_____
_____
_____
_____
_____
_____
_____
_____
_____
_____
_____

෴

There are days when the "what if" needs to look seriously at the "what is."

The outcome of encouraging someone to "try to be like Jesus" brings that individual directly onto the devil's work bench.

෴

The church is not built on assumptions but on applications of Truth.

Assumptions lack proof and lead to conjecture. They bring a false narrative into the picture of the church.

I've met pastors who practice a self-pleasing occupation rather than engaging in a selfless ministry.

⋞⋟

Like Noah, when we are placed somewhere with a "survival kit," we can have the assurance that God is piloting the ship called "A Difficult Time." But be assured, any and all supplies needed have been gathered and He's steering the boat.

⋞⋟

༄༅

There exists a difference between a repentance made from the flesh and one guided by the Spirit nature.

༄༅

❧❧

30 to 40 years ago, the term "balance" was very popular in the church—bad vs. good must be taught in tandum. The Bible is one way to gather teaching, but so are other types helpful. What isn't of God tends to fade away—with some other wrong filling in.

❧❧

≈≈

There is Someone bigger than Covid-19 covering the earth with HIS power.

≈≈

_____
_____
_____
_____
_____
_____
_____
_____
_____
_____
_____
_____
_____

The cross is an implement of punishment and death, not of life. It's an advertisement of death to self.

When the cross became a thing of beauty, it became a "thing" of no spiritual relevance for many.

⁂

For some time, I tried to live Philippians 3:10 . . . knowing Jesus, while sharing His sufferings, and becoming like Him in His death. There always seems a caveat, like suffering, to become the "good" part of the Word.

⁂

_____
_____
_____
_____
_____
_____
_____
_____
_____
_____
_____

Although not stated in the Bible, Queen Esther's life points us to the fact that no matter the days we're in, "we're meant to be for such a time as this." So what is the church doing in "such a time as this"?

⸙

Unlike the ancient city of Jericho with the Israelites marching around their perimeter, the church no longer makes the heart of the unbeliever quiver and melt. (Joshua 2:11)

It's easier to believe the lies that saturate the world than trusting the Word of God spoken in a church

⸙

Genesis 1:1-2 For those who experienced the visit from the Holy Spirit in many churches of the 1960s and are still alive today, will notice the subtle, but purposeful shift away from the teaching of the Word and the silence of the Holy Spirit. Spiritual darkness has slowly encompassed the Word. What will be the outcome? Perhaps a "Let there be . . ." home-going to a new heaven and new earth for all who have stood fast in belief.

The Lord has given us a long period of time in order to become familiar with His Truth. Without much attention given him, Satan has been pecking away at the solid, Word alone, Christ alone teaching.

Satan, knowing that his time is limited, is making the church reflective of the culture—normalizing it with the world is his current ploy.

An idol is something that makes us worried and nervous when it can't be found.

In a society where bars remain open and the church remains closed, we can surmise that we're losing the battle.

Praise is a tool for overcoming what assails us. It is aligning ourselves with the Host of Heaven.

Doing God's will requires the power of the Holy Spirit.

೫ುಲ್

It's interesting; Jesus never mentioned the name of His betrayer.

Many Judases exist in the world today. Just like that last supper, they blend in.

Pilate tried to evade dealing with Jesus. And many of us are no different.

೫ುಲ್

A brick is a self/made object; a biblical example of salvation by works. A stone or rock is God's creation, a picture of the Word. Young David exampled that in 1st Samuel 17. There's no biblical reference that we should likewise toss rocks at people—just the Word of Truth.

As a living stone with a few bricks still in place, we're sometimes chiseled in order to fit us where God wants us. The Holy Spirit poking away at our selves hurts our pride.

I cannot and do not understand the grace, love and mercy of God in my life. But I accept it.

One who strives to be a shepherd to a flock of "sheep" must first know the real Shepherd.

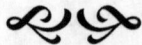

Creator God created the earth in purity only to be invaded by Satan. Why do we not expect Satan to invade God's new "territory"? Especially with new Christians, a new church?

An example: Nehemiah was at work rebuilding a protective wall when a figure of Satan (Sanballat) came along, spreading his fears with words of challenge. A reply from Nehemiah is one I carry in my prayer pocket: "The God of heaven will make us/me prosper . . . but you (Satan) have no portion nor right nor business with me" (Nehemiah 2:20).

It was Good Friday and I watched as my prayers were buried along with my swords of human battle. The whole of it was dead—as were the words of the cantata we in the choir were singing. Then Easter arrived with the singing of "Then Came Sunday"—a resurrection from that which had been dead. But 1st Peter's words that morning were alive with promise as were the words of the music. Oh, the preciousness of God's Word. (1st Peter 1:21) The grave of death had been opened to a new life.

Search for the Word, take heart in that Word, and carry on.

߷

If we must cross the Jordan River in order to reach the "milk and honey" on the other side, many of us would fear the wide swath of river water facing us. Like the Israelites of old, we don't dare trust what the Lord has laid before us. However, we must not fear the pathways of God. If it is crossing some hardships, so be it. It's worth the freshness of the spiritual food waiting on the other side. (Joshua 1:10)

߷

_____

_____

_____

_____

_____

_____

_____

_____

_____

_____

_____

_____

One of the most important parts of Christianity is that we died WITH Christ on that Cross. And it's probably the factor we just can't put into steady belief.

Living the Cross life doesn't happen all at once. It's a steady growth in understanding. And may I add: suffering.

While the people of Noah's day drowned in a sea of disbelief, today too many folks are drowning themselves in a sea of false beliefs.

We rarely hear sermons addressing death to the self, yet that's the only way to live a life with Christ in us, the hope of glory.

The self-life and the biblical Jesus, the Christ in us cannot occupy the same space in our spiritual homes.

The first thing Satan presented to the woman in the garden was a glorification of her self—the nature of the flesh.

Eve had to have been made with a "self" in her. It caved when presented with the idea that she "would be God" if she listened to her visitor. Lucifer's want list of being god was something he had desired and even suggested to Creator God causing the liar to take himself elsewhere.

If we follow the pattern of Satan's "I want to be," and Eve's "I could be" where would we BE?

In order to live Spirit-filled lives, we must die to the self with which we were born.

The self is a tattered "wannabe" that cannot be anything but what it is.

The only way to rid the self from our lives is to take it to the Cross and leave it there.

~~~

Too often the church has been modernized to the point that we no longer know what it really is.

~~~

We'll never know the depths of God's love for us nor His plan for our lives unless we forfeit the self nature and exchange it for the nature of Jesus.

Our spiritual lives, the lives Jesus died to give us, are free to all who not only believe, but are willing to allow the selves we're born with to be taken to the Cross.

Dying to the self is not an overnight accomplishment.

There is more to the Christian walk than removal of sin in one's life. That's the easy part. The difficulty is to desire, be motivated enough, to love the life that God wants us to have; to participate in that new creation.

We're afraid to rid ourselves of the self-nature without knowing what we'll look like afterward.

୬୨

I'm a bit fussy about worship services. I don't want to be entertained, nor hear a joke, nor watch TV. I want to sing of His mercies and listen to the Truth of the Word. In other words—worship.

୬୨

Perhaps we don't think about just how tricky the devil can be. He'll use bits of Scripture to pull us off the walkway designed by the Holy Spirit in order for us to grow in Christ. The pity is thinking we're there when we're not "there" but are actually "done in" by the evil one.

※

At one point in time, Jesus wondered if He would find faith when He returned to earth. (Luke 18:8) That's a thought we should focus on in order to determine if we fit that truth.

※

Conjecture: The only light in hell is through a small hole in the ceiling. Only one item could they see: the cross they spent their earthly days rejecting and furthermore, spitting on the sidewalks toward the One they had the opportunity to believe.

Every sadness, every badness, every rocky cliff, every "I'm drowning in these waters," every "I can't take another blow," every tear shed, I must confess that the God of Heaven has overseen them all for my ultimate benefit.

By the grace of God one of the first things I learned as a new believer was that my "feelings" were not a measure of anything biblical.

⁂

When being "crucified" for telling the Truth, it matters not; I've already been crucified on the Cross of Christ

⁂

Heaven is not the place where we settle our issues with others, especially a husband.

Sometimes the Holy Spirit must "strip" us of our pride. It's like undressing in a store window.

꙰

When walking through the silence of a dark time in life, it took a long while before I could fully trust that the Lord was indeed accompanying me with every step. Sometimes I wondered if an angel was sent along to catch me if I stumbled.

꙰

Today tolerance has become the byway of man's thinking.

It must be difficult for pastors/teachers to write sermons these days with so many differing beliefs in the pews . . . or perhaps from the pulpit itself.

There's a crescendo of power in the depths of our being when the Lord comes to those who wait.

As Jesus walks slowly to greet us, we see His beauty—it's unearthly in its expression of love. I can't help but fall, worshiping the Lord Who gave His life in exchange for mine. His beauty, His glow of joy as He greets me—unworthy as I am. Behold, He comes soon. Oh Lord, how many times did I forsake You and here You stand, waiting to take me home.

According to Malachi, God "hates" false worship, false teaching and the falsities of published works.

Again, from Malachi, as an offering the Lord of creation desires the first fruits from fields and trees, not the hamburger from a sick cow.

Throughout my life, I have found that the Bible is sufficient for every negative or positive action filling my days.

When man transforms his "gold," he reforms it into an image of his choosing. When God transforms His "gold" He restores believers into His likeness and image.

We hear of the grace of God, but without the knowledge of sin and the response of repentance, of what use is it?

Sins are not brought to light to condemn, but to cleanse.

It only took one simple, perhaps pleasant bite to crash the world and its people into a promised death.

The church began in Acts 2 with Peter's first sermon. According to Thessalonians 4:13-17, Paul writes that the church will end when it is raptured. And that may occur at any time.

Looking about and listening to the church at large, it appears that what is new in the Christian's realm is also wrong.

It would appear that the God of Creation, Jesus, was not the god Judas wanted Him to be. There are still those who want to make Jesus over into someone's view of Him. One that isn't so heavenly minded. As was Judas, they're just not getting paid $30 for the effort.

❧

While God's love for us is a matter of His grace; it seems we've made loving God into a law.

❧

_____
_____
_____
_____
_____
_____
_____
_____
_____
_____
_____
_____

❧❧

A person suffering during lengthy trails needs to know that one can be powdered with God's grace to soften the blows. It does hurt to suffer, but it really is worth the trial.

If a "new" practice or belief comes into the church, let it be known that it's just Satan wearing a disguise.

It's the work of those who know the Word to pray Satan out the door.

❧❧

Whomever we wrong will wear the face of God until we right the situation.

One can have ministry in the heart but not in the hand. One can also have ministry in hand but not in the heart.

It is not easy for Christians to learn God's way, His way. Human Nature isn't God's nature.

Sermon title: "If God isn't all Who He says He is in His Word, why are we sitting there?"

❧❧

Through thousands of years of biblical history, from its first pages to its last, the underlying focus of the Bible is aimed at the days we currently have set before us.

❧❧

On a daily basis, Jesus will turn the water of ordinary happenings into the wine of a new creation in His followers. (John 2:1-11)

Each miracle of God has an inner spiritual truth attached to it.

Woe to those who attend a church service, but don't need nor want the Lord of it.

Two bodies of water, the Red Sea and the Jordan River were dried by the Lord in order to bring thousands of people into a better life. What waters have stood between me and God's purpose in life? Why am I reluctant to stick my toes in any barrier between the Lord and me?

What situation in life would we like the Lord to "dry up" so that we may cross over from one of Satan's strongholds into the promised "land" of His Word?

Consciousness of sin creates a climate of works.

False teachers: ADD to the Word; SUBTRACT from the deity of Jesus; MULTIPLY requirements for salvation, and DIVIDE congregations.

⊰⊱

Water baptism is not the means of rebirth. They're two separate events.

⊰⊱

Dying to self is impossible using the self as the hatchet.

It is difficult if not impossible to be rooted in Christ while still watering the roots of self.

In this last age, it is not so important that we, the church, be reformed as it is that Jesus be formed in each of us.

The call of the believer is not to live and then die, but to die and then live.

Whether Satan is accusing us of sin or encouraging us TO sin, he always appeals to the flesh nature. So the more we die to the self, the less Satan has to work with.

The Old Testament covenant was based on living right.
The New Testament covenant is based on believing right.

⁂

There are times when we experience the most powerful enemy of faith. It's fear.

⁂

If we hold hands with the world long enough, we might as well go steady.

Today Bibles are being published that are nothing more than paraphrased, opinionized works of folly.

I hadn't noticed until recently that by some method, the church has raised itself above the Lord of it.

It occurs to me that the more I allow my self to die, the more the room I have for Jesus.

Walking in the Word has its benefits. The Word is the only place where we find the face of God.

It seems that sin is no longer a "worry" in the church. It is an act committed toward God and man that cannot be undone by ignoring it.

What beautiful scenery (lessons) have I not enjoyed as a result of going "my way" not fully trusting His way.

It isn't the length of time that we've lived on this earth that matters but the content of its living.

We are living in a period of time where it's a choice between discernment and deception. One will glorify Him; the other might not end within God's favor.

Many are we who honor Jesus with our lips, but not our lives.

The ancient Jews awaited a Son of David, a King Who would rule in peace and righteousness. There also existed the Son of Man idea, one who would rule over all kingdoms of the world. What they didn't expect was a suffering, cross nailed figure who carried a new message.

What are our expectations of the Savior God Who will one day come again?

❧❦

I'm determined to live in the arms of faith, not yoked to the stiffness of fear. It's easier said than done.

❧❦

We are a thirsting world—much of it self-fulfilling. When that supply runs dry, and it will, the Lord will replace those self-thirsts into a thirsting after Jesus.

Is our emphasis on the spirit of the age or on the Spirit of truth? It's a relevant choice to make. And soon.

Mary was impregnated with the spirit of joy, hope, peace, good will, grace, peace, blessings, etc. So will we be if we commit our lives to the Cross of Christ and His Word.

Just thinking: If we are the bride and Jesus the groom, I know of no instance where a bridegroom puts his beloved bride through torture before he comes to get her. He loves her and protects her. Again, just wondering.

It has been said that history repeats itself. In today's world that would be the "let us" of the Towers of Babel. And that was after a cleansing world-wide flood. There are churches, businesses, and ordinary people who think we're too powerful to suffer something like a fire. People "can" survive a flood, but not a fire, the one spoken of in 2nd Peter 3:3-7. Knowing that fact should send every believer to the friend, relative or foe who doesn't know what the future holds. In the day of the fire, the earth will run out of places to hide.

~~~

In the days I have left here on earth, please Lord, help me and make me to become that which you want me to be.

~~~

Sometimes I wish a "dumb ass" would speak to a few wayward folks in the church. Maybe they'd listen to the donkey; they haven't been listening to the Word.

(1st Peter 5:8-9) I for one, do not want to contribute to the size of Satan's roaring lion's belly. In today's world that roar is louder than the bell of the church.

Do not "curse" or pout about trials and sufferings; they are the Holy Spirit's implement to bring about His purpose for our lives. At times, the type of trial is a means of showing us what we're worshiping that is in the false bracket.

There are those days in life when I've wanted to hear the Carpenter's last nail being pounded into my home in the heavens.

The reason the Holy Spirit takes us on so many Word Walks is to see the face of God in them.

Whenever hardening of our spiritual arteries sets in, Satan's attack will come on the flesh nature.

If it's a new "way" that is being taught, through "How to" books as an example, be assured it's not God's way. Replacement Theology was a very popular example of this factor.

At a writers conference in the '80s, we were told the following: "If you want to be published, you MUST write a 'How to' book as that's what's popular."

No one needs to ask oneself if one has been born again. That individual will KNOW. A different Spirit, with different thinking, behaving has come into oneself.

If we are earnestly seeking the Lord's ways, we'll be taken apart via the Holy Spirit's sanctifications and then slowly rebuilt into the image and likeness of Jesus. So keep on keeping on.

Jesus asked these four study-worthy questions: "Where are you? What do you seek? What can I do for you? Whom do you seek?"

∽∽

Sweet Jesus, Thou has been like the sun, blazing upon my neck, burning into my soul and then setting, hiding Your face from my consciousness while imparting Your warmth on others. Now, I will turn like the earth once again to the hotness of Your Word that it may burn out the sin in my life and cause new growth in order that the fruit of that growth might nurture not only me but others. Grant me this grace. Thank you, Lord Jesus.

∽∽

www.ingramcontent.com/pod-product-compliance
Lightning Source LLC
Chambersburg PA
CBHW071901290426
44110CB00013B/1230